THAT ONE MOMENT

**A collection of Poetry, and Photography
By W. Robert Winston**

THAT ONE MOMENT

ISBN: 978-0-578-20491-8

Printed in USA by 48HrBooks (www.48HrBooks.com)

Dedication

There are many who deserve this dedication, but we can narrow this book to three special ladies:

*My mother, **Claudette Winston**, whose love and encouragement kept me focused on being committed and dedicated to producing this book;*

*In memory of my grandmother, **Dorothy Smith**, for her spiritual guidance and love towards her family;*

*In memory of my aunt, **Beatrice Simmons**, who encouraged me to be a writer at a young age, with countless phone calls, mailing and editing my short stories, I honor you for your spirit is embedded in this book.*

Also, a shout out to the Stuyvesant Heights Christian Church, Brooklyn, NY; the staff and students (past and present) of the Ronald Edmonds Learning Center – M.S. 113K; and to my members/alumni of Non-Stop Production (NSP Youth, Inc.). Hoping this book inspires and motivates the youth to do great things.

Finally, a special thank you to Mr. Scott Konrad and Ms. Wednesday Webb for reviewing this and for all the sound advice you gave that allowed me to complete this book!

Table of Contents

Foreword
by Donna Coulter

Poetry, like a branch in the wind has the flexibility to teach, inspire, touch, and awaken the soul. The poems in this book were written to remind us of our past and to keep us grounded along our journeys.

This collection of poems will enlighten the clouded mind, clarify the blurred vision, and nurture the spirit of the reader.

Each poem will find its way into your life, just the way "you" need it to.

Mr. Wayne R. Winston has welcomed us on this expedition of pride, love and perseverance. Mr. Winston's style and tone expresses the "just right" ingredients needed to reach an audience from the youth to elders. Mr. Winston's ongoing passion to inspire young people about African-American culture, music, pride and dignity is displayed in his poetic style. Open your mind and let the words in this book speak to your heart.

Preface

From a young age, I have involved myself in the arts from music, to visual arts, photography, and creative writing. This book is a 25-year collection of poetry, and a few personal quotes, which reflects many of my experiences of life.

You will notice that some poems are dated, based on my daily "moments", and special events I've been blessed to take part in. Some are emotional, and even long-winded, as some were written during hospital stays, fighting illness, and making life decisions. Others are a sign of the times, as we look at victories, loses, blessings, deaths, life-long journeys, and reflecting on "that one moment", when it all changes.

As an artist, I wanted to include my photography, with photos of special moments, family, and friends that may connect with selected poems.

Outside of recording and releasing music, this is the first of perhaps many more writings I hope to present for the public to enjoy.

Peace and Blessings!
W. Robert Winston

THAT
ONE
MOMENT

I

TIME

HELLO

Woke up and stretched
Watched the sun arise from its bed
Looked out the window and said "Good Morning"
But not a word was said.
Should I expect an answer?
Perhaps the sunny greeting was enough.
I put a smile on my face
And the wind blew a kiss without a fuss
It was just morning
But the day was complete
All I could say was "Thanks"
And let the Spirit guide my feet.

10/23/01

POPPA

The father figure;

> As I sit and listen
> I sit and learn
> Words to discern
>
> In the moment when the Lord anointed you
> And the village appointed you
> Speak teacher
> Speak Father
> Thank you, Poppa

- Dedicated to my mentors,
  Baba Jitu Weusi
  Elder Carey Richardson
  Elder Herbert Johnson

FIRST LADY

My mom
My first true love to teach me such
How to live
How to give
How to lose
How to win
How to fly
How to soar
I give back to the one I adore

A love that was meant for me
You're my First Lady
Oh, how I love thee.

4-U-N-I-2-B-1
(For You and I to be One)

It takes one to give
One to receive
One to hold and accept
The other must believe

It takes one to speak
One to listen
One can dream
If the other has vision

It takes one to touch
For the other to feel
But it takes two to love
And know when it's real

1/7/15

THAT ONE MOMENT (PART I: LOVE)

Took this one moment,
to stop and breathe,
A break in the day,
just to enjoy the spring.
A time to reflect,
on the sight before my eyes.
It was your grace and beauty,
that took me by surprise.

Perhaps I wasn't really there;
perhaps I stopped too soon,
Before I can hear the pretty voice,
that sent the vibes throughout the room.

Maybe I didn't know my direction,
but your friendship allowed me to see.
You gave me courage to stop,
and take this one moment,
to stop and breathe.

4/18/08

HEY SON

Had a chat with my Father this morning...

Like every morning, I gave Him thanks for what He's done for me.
>   But this day seemed different; there was so much on my mind.
>   I had to talk to my Father, I needed Him at this time.
>   On bended knee, I prepared for prayer.
>   Feeling His presence, it was in the air.
>   I called His name, but I couldn't go on.
>   For at that moment, I heard a voice... my Father respond.

And He said, "Hey Son..."

>   I know this life has been a struggle, but yet I must say.
>   You've come this far by faith. My, you've come a mighty long way.

>   I've seen your tears, and I've seen your joy
>   I've seen your fear; I've seen your sorrow.
>   But I know your past, your present, and I'll be here to help you face tomorrow.

"Hey son..."

>   What's in your heart?
>   You've fed my sheep, and you've stood firm on my Word,
>   Your family boasts about you, even strangers who've never heard.
>   Though others may complain about the way they live
>   You speak of hope, peace, and the love I have to give
>   See, in times of trouble, you would call my name
>   And as we celebrate, you still do the same.

"Hey son…"

You've climbed mountains you've never faced before,
But the best is yet to come, and there is more to endure
You stand tall and proud, so you continue your mission.
Not many are strong enough to stand in your position

For they said the road is rough and the going gets tough
But you manage to keep the faith, and that's more than enough
    At times you may fall short,
But if you remember to hold on to my unchanging hand,
Remind others to do the same, and Stand.

That's all I have to say for now, I see you have much to do
"Hey son…"
Go! For now, my Power is within you.

There was silence in the room; it was the start of a new day,
For the time was at hand, the Father has sent me on my way.

So as I walked away, he called me back.
My Father called out, "Hey son…"
Before you go, I wanted to say I love you,
And by the way, "A job well done!"

5/5/02

WHAT IF

Have you ever had a thought…

Have you ever cared…

Have you ever loved…

Have you ever dared…

Have you ever dreamed…

Have you ever danced…

Have you ever lived life…

Have you ever taken a chance…

What if…

It never happened at all?

1/29/13

QUOTE…

"Don't let a bad five minutes ruin your 24 hours".

LITTLE STEPS

What makes a child smile?
What makes a dream revealing?
What makes a life content?
What makes love appealing?
It's just that one moment, *one step at a time*.

MAMA'S LOVE

The first heartbeat
The first kiss
The first love
Still her perfect gift

Given little time
Her works unseen
Her voice I yearn to hear
From princess to Queen

My hero, my star
Her shine
Seen afar
My love from birth
You're the precious gift to mother earth

Thank You Mama

1/8/15

II

VISIONS

QUOTE...

"Your life isn't centered around your excuses; it should be built on your purposes."

STILL TOGETHER

Yes, here we are, once again

Where these crossroads once met. Remember me?

We were blind, but now we see.

They said we couldn't get this far

We look up, there's that shining star.

But yet... People don't understand who we are.

Who we are?

We were Kings and Queens from long ago

From Slaves to Servants, from to and fro.

From the beginning of time

Through valleys, to the hills, and all through the storm.

From ancestors who suffered from the day they were born.

They try to hold us down, but we made a dream come true.

Seventy-Five Years, it's because of people like you.

It was faith that got us here, cause we held on to this vision

And those from long ago, with pain and ambition.

Through fighting and suffering, that's my people.

From bondage to freedom, that's my people

From tribulations to victory, that's my people

From struggle to endurance, that's my people.

Breaking our backs, to breaking down walls, that's my people

We're still together

See, here we are, once again

Where these crossroads once met.

BUT MY PEOPLE...

We still haven't finished yet.

They say we must lift as we climb and leave no one behind.

We continue this journey and press on through time

But now is the time we go our separate ways

Looking back one more time at our glorious days.

See you at the next crossroad.

My heart be with you forever.

As long as that Spirit dwells within you,

Remember... We're still together.

11/7/03

FLY

I rose above the clouds for the first time
Heaven above earth
I watch the mist flow in the wind
Across the mountainside
Where a new life begins

A new fall breeze
The swaying of trees
Telling me stories
Of their mighty stand
On God's territory

Wishing I was an eagle
Soaring to the highest peak
So I can be closer to God
Awaiting for Him to speak

I soar higher and higher
And the pressure of doubt
Only heightens my curiosity
On what this life is about

Though time is not my friend
But a mere companion on this flight
No dreams, but visions
One final goal in sight

Let the sun rise and lead the way
Let the sun shine another day
No turning back
Let me be
Let me fly
Set me free

1/8/15

QUOTE...

"Life is good as long as you have it... Eternal life is better as long as you earn it."

SOUNDS OF MUSIC

I listen for the beat, the sounds of the drums with fire
The cymbals are heard, for it cries out as the fire burns
I beat the drums with passion
With mellow sounds that surrounds as the world turns

The trumpets flare, a piano key so low.
I witness the music of the spirit
And rhythms carry as we go

Controlling each sound with grace
All so pleasing to the ear
I play my music with pride
With courage and still, no fear.

For whom I play for, is not for some to understand
For I envision the sounds of life, no ordinary tempo for man
Some songs may end, never again to be heard in the wind
But this music is everlasting from the heart within

10/21/01

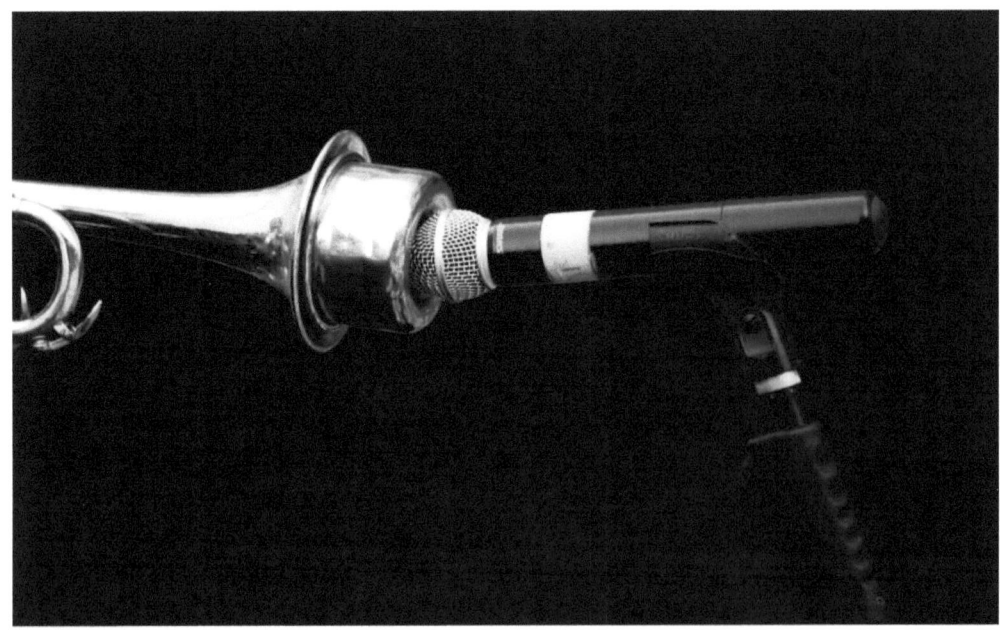

COLORS

The essence of crimson red flows through the veins of a city
As a golden sunset fades into a sea of blue
The night falls slowly over the pale sandy beach
As the waves come ashore reflecting the moon's hue

A lonely bird perched in a tree
Watching the fall colored leaves descend to their final resting place
Like a mother hoping her child comes home
Awaiting the sun to shine upon her face

Seeing a world, living dreams
In a great city of flashing lights that rule the night
To vision a full moon,
That enlightens a snow-covered road beyond the sight

We walk a bridge to a new beginning
Hand in hand, let's watch each moment at its best
And be adrift with the stars til they fade away
Sharing a joy of colors with the time that's left

1/5/15

LIVE THE DREAMS OF A STAR

I'm just another star in the sky.
Like all stars, we have dreams.
To be a shooting star for the world to see.

So as my journey begins, where my destination lies, I don't know.
As I streak through the sky, not knowing where I'll go.

While blazing through the sky, I see stars like me, friends, some new, some
old.
All who have traveled through their time, with stories to be told.

But like the dreams of children, who look towards the heavens for a star.
Let a star shine bright with dignity, pride, and hope...telling them who they
are.

So as a shooting star, I search for my destiny, knowing my journeys must
come to an end.
I fall from the heavens, now you see me descend.
Don't worry about where my journey ends, just look at where I've been.

Live the dreams of a star, through strife, pain, and sorrow.
Beyond the limits, reach for the stars, and together, we'll face tomorrow.

Live the dreams of a star. Don't be afraid, you're not alone.
Following the stars across the sky, because they will guide you home.

Live the dreams of a star to be all that you can be.
And when you descend to your destiny, fill your heart with love, and Be Free!

11/14/93

*(Originally written for the youth of Non-Stop Production; first published in "Of
Sunshine and Daydreams" by The National Library of Poetry – 1996)*

THAT ONE MOMENT (PART II: LIFE)

I remember the days coming home from school
With food on the table, living by grandma's rules

Yeah, I had the life, so simple for a child
Homework, then tv, and my mom coming home with a smile

But that mode was temporary
May I spread my wings and soar on this new journey

From a boy to a man, I can't see tomorrow,
But I can only dream
Never knew how far I can go
Just ain't what it seems
They say the world today isn't what it used to be

People without homes, kids dying in the streets
Mothers selling babies, just to find a spot to eat.

Street corners get flooded by kids on the run
You either rap, play ball, or die by the gun

Now we in the days when educated fools can get over
No matter how hard you try, the world stays colder

Who wanna change the game, change the fame
In a world where people don't even know your name.

Can't judge you by your color,
That's not my mission
Can your talk right, can you walk right,
Can you stand tall, can you endure the fight
The world got you in that position.
Everyone wants change, but they're afraid to be heard.
These people got you hooked by every word

You could talk a good game, and put yourself to the test
You don't need a crowd to tell you that you're the best

Regardless of the game, it's still my move
I take the next step, in a blink of an eye.
Folks think I failed, but I'll just take one more try.

Who's with me; sometimes we gotta roll the dice, take a chance.
It's win or lose in this final dance

But who told you to give up, that's not in the plan
This is you time now, to grow from a boy to a man.

You have a voice, you age don't matter
Your size don't matter
Your education does matter
Not your style and your status
All weapons come against you and I,
Verbal shots coming at us

Hold my hand child.
We're in this together
You were never left alone
In this to win this, it's all for the better.

Just think, where your mind can take you
Leaving your mental footprints in the background

Looking forward to tomorrow
You speak life about tomorrow
You believe in tomorrow
I know both you and I have the power to change tomorrow.

2/17/14

THE SEED

Watered and nurtured

In darken form, no light to view

The time was written for another moment

Frozen within the mist and dew

Not broken, but awaken to the dawn of a new day.

Until the new midnight hour begins

Born again in victory

Final moment, the last one.

JAZZ

Soul of the Vibe

Feel the live sounds of the town

I walk through listening to every note that's going down

Reflections of the stars long gone.

Waiting for Miles to play that song.

We ride the SoulTrane with Coltrane

With the beats from Max and Art,

This music can not fall apart

And we drift to the voice of Ella

Rocking to Calloway, the smooth-looking fella.

Big bands, 20 men deep, The Duke takes the stage

And through the side curtains we peep.

Let's watch the Lady sing the blues,

Let the Bird spread the news.

NOW'S THE TIME!

So as Lester Leaps In, let the music begin

Yet it still continues, jazz still lives today

Let's go to the club to see Wynton play.

With tunes of yesterday

With the spirit of Louis and the passion of Monk

The fire and desire that gives us a feel for Dizzy,

For that's JAZZ, and this music is still with me.

2/12/04

THAT ONE MOMENT (PART III: HOPE)

It was a new day, but not the same as many others
Reflecting on my fallen sisters and brothers
I took a walk to think on the one moment in time
Streets still in silence, and still no peace of mind

Thinking there was no hope, but hope wasn't far away
Looking for a sign, something to brighten my day.
The smoke still rose, and blew across the sky,
As I watch lost souls in the street ask why.

As my journey stopped me at the corner,
I can feel the rumble of that big red engine passing by.
Awaiting its next mission, no sirens, no speed, it was at peace.
At least for the moment.
She rode on by, turning the corner, as its passengers looked out
the windows in wonder.
Knowing what was left behind,
Streets no longer in silence, but yet perhaps, some peace of mind
The fireman smiled, with a grin not so loud,
Perhaps a glimmer of hope, enough to make me proud.

9/12/01

BLUES

Lonely days lay beside me
Holding hands with the memories of you not here
Looking for a sign to wake up from a dream
But remain trapped behind the wall of a single tear

I finally knew the obvious
While listening to the final notes of your song
Waiting for a door to open, and the sun to set
But already knew that you were gone

I could have given you my heart
My spirit
My soul
My Life
But all you needed was my time
All you wanted was to be loved
As do I

Lonely days now lay beside me
Holding hands with the memories of you not here
Looking for a sign to wake up from a dream
But remain trapped behind the wall of a single tear

1/2/15

BLACK & WHITE

It's my skin versus your skin
I was taught not to hate you
You was told how to hate me

To learn HATE is a fall from grace
As a learn to love in a different place
Perhaps a different space to set us apart
So our minds can disconnect from the vilest of the world
And perhaps one day return to birthplace of
> Freedom
> Peace
> Joy
> Respect
> Unity
> Love

And eyes connect for I must look past a darken spirit;
That hasn't been taught the true meaning of life
Whatever dwells in the spirit is listening through the eyes
And seeing thoughts of the mind and soul
Putting me in a place where I don't want to be
But in a place God needs me to be.
What must you say…

BEYOND THE WALLS

I stand face to face with the world before my eyes
Looking for my dreams to rise
My eyes on the prize.
But between me and that prize, there lies the truth,
about being black in this society, things I've learned from my youth

See, may I talk in this circle? I hope you're willing to listen;
For beyond the walls, there are ears that are still missing.
Perhaps for the better, it's not hard to understand,
because beyond that wall, there's a boy who refuses to be a man

And there's a girl so flirtatious, she can never walk through that door
Until she's on the brink of death, and experience things she never seen
before.
See, beyond these walls, there's hatred and racism,
Continuous of days long gone,
Another generation before us, and I let my words continue on.

Respect to the past, we lack, suffer forgotten generations
Who were killed in the cotton fields, and died for an education,
And when 41 shots ring out,
There is no respect for the black nation
From the streets of hip-hop, to a land of kings and queens
I see the visions of struggle, and beyond the walls,
That's they way they want it to be.

We break through the walls of slavery
and step into century of bravery
But I still fall into the pain of society, don't lie to me.
You can't be like them, so don't try to be!

See, out there, society would like to stop this message I send you.
And I reply…
Oh, did the color of my skin offend you?

Well I guess it did, cause even my people can't see,
what's the connection of being black, and being free.
Now I must break down the walls, for this game can't be played,
When you fight against a people of a darker shade.

See, I'm in it to win it, 'til death do us part.
I hope you're in it too, unless you have no heart.

Are you trapped in, surrounded wall to wall?
For if you press hard enough, the enemies are bound to fall.
We're still locked in a prison, our minds in a daze.
Cause we've been mis-educated, don't be surprised or amazed.

If you can hear me in this circle, by now you should have learned
Beyond the walls, you take my message, for now it's your turn.
You see, it's you who must spread the words and you can't hold back.
For beyond the walls deep within, is the meaning of being black.

2/22/03

III

Journey

QUOTE...

"Knowledge is a game seldom played by the ignorant and the unwise."

BEGINNINGS

My child, where are you?

I know you're not lost

I know where you are, you shining star,

Mom and dad have taught you well

With a heart of gold, you're special, can't you tell?

The picture seems clear, that's why I search for you.

This job of mine is complete,

but you still have more to do.

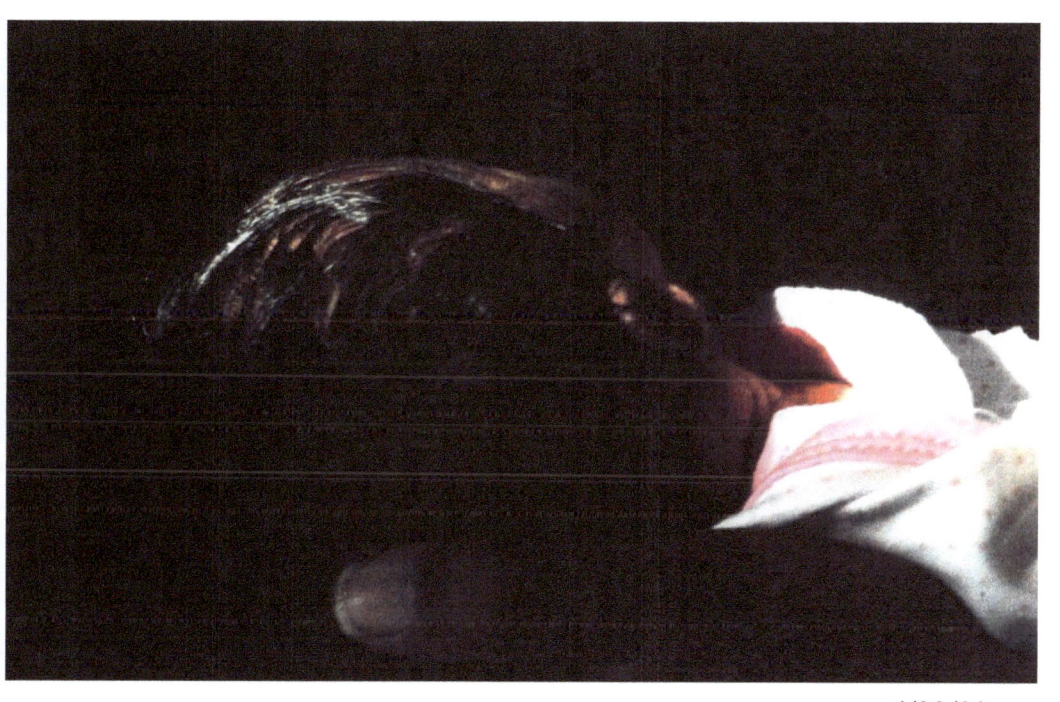

4/22/03

THE WIND STILL BREATHES

It's just the spirit of my ancestors
Encouraging me as I go through the day
Pushing me along the way

It's the spirit of my ancestors
Reminding me of where I stand
The ones who told me "Yes I Can!"

It's the spirit of my ancestors
Who once walked the earth
Who valued and showed me how much I was worth

It's the spirit of my ancestors
That I felt in the wind
Knowing their presence is with me until the end

It's the spirit of my ancestors
That walked that freedom trail
To fight for justice and equality for all to prevail

It's the spirit of my ancestors
I feel in my sleep
As I pray to the Lord, bless the souls he keeps

It's spirit of my ancestors
I feel when the sun goes away
Reminds me, though the body's gone, their love is here to stay

It's the spirit of my ancestors
For now they are free
All in God's plan, how it was meant to be

1/5/15

SMILE

Just take the moment
It may never come again
No second chance in the preview
Just a moment to see you

Feeling a summer breeze,
Your vibe is in the wind
The greeting I long for
A love I search for

But it starts with this one moment
Face to face
Looking for your smile
For that special place
In my heart

1/1/15

THAT ONE MOMENT (PART IV: CHANGE)

Rise Up

Stand Strong

Same Music

Same Song

Quiet Peace

New Day

Only Perfection

Your Way

Time Moves

New Born

Birds Sing

Days Gone

New Hope

Time Alone

Only Love

Carries On

Big Dreams

Only Try

Believe once

Never Die

Rise Up

Stand Strong

Peace of Mind

New Song

1/17/13

COLORED

I've been born
Which road do I choose?
Do I struggle to win?
Or do I fight, just to lose

Do I give in to the hate?
Do I choose my fate?
Do I stand like Martin and Malcolm
Can I endure this debate?

Do I break every chain?
Or put locks on the chains of fear
And cast them away
Enough to disappear

Do I allow another man to define myself?
I can't
God put me in this position
Can't rely on anyone else

Do I stay in the shadows?
And stop others from moving on
While enemies keep praying
For the day that I'm gone

Do I run like a slave?
Accept pain on demand
I won't give in or fall
Because yes, I'm still a man

Tell the children to live
Give these little boys some direction
Tell these mothers to find real fathers
To be their daughters' protection

Don't sacrifice my blood for nothing
That's not what I need
My true color of blackness
That's the color I bleed

Can I speak to my people?
For all must see
Until we have peace, love, and unity,
We'll never be free

If I rise with the sun
Then let me set with the moon
Say a prayer for the martyrs
Who died too soon

Do I survive on faith?
Do I rely on hope?
When I trust and believe
God's will allow me to cope

No time to dwell
Or complain about the plan
For when the day I was born
Is where my journey began

1/5/15

QUOTE...

"Watching time go by is like asking a question in an empty room".

I stood on the sand watching the calm sea,
Looking at the wonders that stood before me.
Perhaps a change was at hand, but that wasn't my plan.
It was God who put me here,
So what should I fear?
I guess it remains to be seen.

You may ponder life and the challenges ahead
Even regret words you may have said
Through the stress of it all, I see we're still standing
And in times like these, life is very demanding
But yet, it remains to be seen.

For there's a time to laugh and a time to cry.
Friends come and go, and time will pass us by.
And the burdens of this world still seem heavy,
You still ask why?
Patience my friend,
This is one moment in time
One moment to remember
This journey continues, as the Spirit dwells within you.
Don't fear the future, for that time will be gone too.
There's a world out there before you and me.
And yet, it remains to be seen.

And as I stood in the sand watching the calm sea,
Wondering what plan God had laid out for me,
The answer was as clear as day,
So I couldn't let this moment slip away
For the best is yet to come,
And this work before us is not quite done;
for it remains to be seen.

As presented to Rev. Cornelius Brown and family
Stuyvesant Heights Christian Church 16th Pastoral Anniversary
5/4/03

TIME

Time did not wait for me
Time was lost and found
I wait for time to agree with my situations
But I'd let it go by without hesitation

I'd walked the edge of time, waiting for life to be
      placed on hold
While others rushed through this game of life
And others stuck in the past letting the countdowns
      control their next move
Still I had nothing to prove

Nothing to say as my 24 came down to none
Time had won
Still, another chance, another day
But time had nothing to say

We make the best of our problems, and the worst of
      our happiness
And no time to waste, yet no time to rest
Another moment gone, new day, but not the same
Realizing time never knew my name.

IV

AMEN

THAT ONE MOMENT (PART V: FAITH)

Searching for direction of who I am
A sign of hope
For the quietness of patience was at hand
Wait with me

Deep are the roads that time forgotten though
Destination unknown, yet we go.
Walk with me

I wait for a voice to tell me I'm forgiven
To never give up a life that is still worth living
For battles lie before us and my heart and soul become my
weapon of choice
Yet I yearn to hear your voice
Talk with me

All my fears are gone, my life will carry on
My head held high, the prize before my eyes
Believe with me

Never fail, never fall
Let me remain strong as I fight for all
Stand with me

SOUL

A Hero don't wear fancy clothes or fly through the skies
They just manage to give their heart and their spirit never dies
Their time and their love may mean a lot to some
Whatever I gave, I'm still satisfied
If it only helped out just one.

I was willing and able and could never say "No"
And God even challenged me to go where no one would go
Trouble tried my patience, and took me down for the count
But the Soul of this Hero would never bow out.

My life seems incomplete at times, but I manage to do my best
But I'm reminded by those TV interruptions, "This Is Only A Test."
I can walk through the valley even in my finest hour
I'll even climb the tallest hill, for the Lord will still give me Power.

May the words of my mouth be a light for some to learn
No matter how dark it may seem, my candle somewhere still burns.
Whether it's in your heart, there's a Hero still there for you
My Soul is a gift from God and together we'll see this through.

10/20/01

CHOOSE YE THIS DAY

I took this moment just to say yes
No fanfare
No celebration
No hype
Just determination

A higher calling
Perhaps this moment was right
To accept who I am
And what I've become
To stand and prepare to walk
From a former self God will move me from

My heart sacrificed to a Holy power unexplained
No regrets and no doubt, a bigger reward now to gain
For I choose this day to make my mark
And take my place from out the dark
For all to hear and see
A gift is here for you and me
This day
It shall be.

HOME

Wherever this road leads

To a place I can call

Home

A place of peace

To be free of the everyday grind

Looking to free my mind

A home where love welcomes you at the door

And the invitation remains open for

Those who seek the comforts of life

Knowing I'm blessed with place of rest

This Home must be God's best.

THAT ONE MOMENT (PART VI: PEACE)

Lost and Found
Heaven Bound

Was Mentally Blind
Now with a Spiritual Mind

Mercy and Grace
Still a smile on my face

For this one life to live
There's more I have to give

Another day to begin
Let your spirit dwell within

And this day too, shall pass
Let your love forever last

The night, too, shall come
Life fulfilled and done

Yet, still I have Peace

1/1/15

QUOTE…

"Why worry about tomorrow… It'll be gone the day after."

THANK YOU

Had to stop by for this one moment.
It's a new day, but it's always good when the time is new
When you spend a special moment with friends like you
New time, another moment we have yet to face.
And it was God who put us in this place.

So why not share this time together,
For moments like these don't last forever.
But first I must reflect on why we're here
Because things aren't the same as it was last year.

Even years before, we can't ignore.
You were there from the start, and here we are once more.
When situations arose, I remember you were there.
When friends walked away, I looked back, and you were still here.
And when pain and suffering came, you showed no fear.
And phone calls at night, just to say how much you care.

A friendship like this, you can't break it
Others may try to fake it.
Even in the bad times, we can still make it.
There were days we were down, feeling unappreciated
Got love for each other, but yet we're still hated
Only two words I need to say, they're not complicated
For my choice of words, they may be few
All that I'd come here for is to say *"Thank You!"*

5/2/04

60

THE BEST IS YET TO COME

Despite the things around us
As hopeless as things may seem
As fear hovers like a cloud
A feeling of lost inside a dream

Or maybe our patience is gone
As we await a voice in our mind
To tell us to love one another
When the world is not so kind

Through gloomy days and restless nights
Brokenhearted and weary soul
For He said we would not be forsaken
Still, my God is in control

And as the sun sets in its faded view
And the stars unite the sky as one
I await that one moment when I'm finally home
For the best is yet to come.

4/22/18

THAT ONE MOMENT (PART VII: FOREVER)

I may not be here with you
I may be a whisper in the wind
I fear the unknown
And with this ending, I must begin
Only time walks beside me
For I may be away for just a while
I may not be around to see your face
Or hold your hand when you smile
If I'm still a memory,
A simple thought,
Or a tear when you weep,
Just remember my love for you
Will always be yours to keep.

1/29/13

PHOTOGRAPHY HISTORY

Book cover: Sunset view of Hudson River, shot from window of Long Island College Hospital, 2006

1. "Hello": Cloudy Sunset in Staten Island, 2008
2. "First Lady": BW photo of mother, Claudette Winston, 2011
3. "4UNI2B1": Wedding photo of Kevin and Dia Bryant, Detroit, MI, 2008
4. QUOTE: Manhattan Sunset View from Brooklyn Bridge, 2014
5. "Little Steps": Photo shoot of Olivia Geters-Cummings, 2006
6. "Mama's Love" Photo of mother and son, "Chantal and Ayinde Eustache at International African Arts Festival, Brooklyn, 2011
7. QUOTE: Supermoon in NYC, 2014
8. "Sounds of Music": Trumpet at Work, Restoration Plaza, Brooklyn, 2014
9. "The Seed": A Growth in the Concrete" – Brooklyn Bridge Park, 2009
10. "Jazz" Saxophone on Stage, International African Arts Festival, Brooklyn, NY 2015
11. "That One Moment: HOPE": Cropped photo of Fire Engine, 2010
12. QUOTE: "Deer at Bronx Zoo, 2011
13. "Beginnings": Photo of granddaughter, Emani Epps, 1 day old, 2010
14. QUOTE: "Sunset on Vanderbilt Ave., Brooklyn, NY, 2012
15. "That One Moment: Forever": Sunset at Hudson River, 2014

www.ingramcontent.com/pod-product-compliance
Lightning Source LLC
Chambersburg PA
CBHW041147250626
47164CB00013B/15